# *NANTUCKET*

## The Delaplaine
## 2022
## Long Weekend Guide

No business listed in this guide has provided *anything* free to be included.

## Andrew Delaplaine

Senior Writer - **James Cubby**

Cover Photo by Ruthie J Miller from Pixbay

# *NANTUCKET*
## The Delaplaine
## Long Weekend Guide

## TABLE OF CONTENTS

# Chapter 1
# WHY NANTUCKET?

Nantucket was once the "whaling capital of the world," and as such was the place where incredible fortunes were created. You can see some of the stately mansions erected by whaling entrepreneurs of the past, some of which have been converted into inns and B&Bs where you can stay the night, living for a little while in the same surroundings they did.

These days, however, the whalers are lost in the mists of history and legend, replaced by hoards of tourists that descend on the island in the prime summer season.

I always like to go to Nantucket (or places like Cape Cod or the Hamptons) just *before* the season or just *after* it. The weather's just as excellent, the difficulty getting into restaurants nonexistent, the shops and beaches less crowded.

But, you go when you can, of course, and for many, that means summer.

Besides enjoying the old mansions, attractions like the **Whaling Museum**, the cobblestone streets, the cedar shake houses, the romantic restaurants, the harborside pubs where you can share a pint with the locals, you get to take in the areas of the island that remain completely pristine. You get to enjoy the windswept seascapes, cranberry bogs, freshwater ponds, salt marshes.

Nantucket is home to a lot of wealthy people, but you can be right beside them, whether you stay overnight or are just making a day-trip out of it.

As with any tourist town, there are a lot of tourist traps and crappy restaurants, but you'll find good selections here that will not lead you astray.

# Chapter 2
# GETTING ABOUT

## GETTING TO THE ISLAND:

You can get over to Nantucket by air (try Nantucket Air, Cape Air or Jet Blue). Other small regional services operate in the busier summer months.

Or you can travel by ferry:

**HY-LINE CRUISES**
34 Straight Wharf, Nantucket, 508-228-3949
www.hylinecruises.com
This is a passenger-only cruise line traveling between Nantucket and Hyannis. Moderate rates. Cruises leaving several times daily. Schedule varies by season.

## THE STEAMSHIP AUTHORITY
508-477-8600
www.steamshipauthority.com/visitors/nantucket
This is the largest ferry service that travels to the
Islands of Martha's Vineyard and Nantucket from
Cape Cod. Frequent daily departures are offered for
passengers, groups, autos, and trucks. Travel dock to
dock in just an hour. Spacious seating on board with
snack bars, free Wi-Fi and TV. Schedule varies by
season.

## GETTING AROUND THE ISLAND

You will not need a car. A lot of people use bikes to
get around, or scooters. Taxis are available, but the
**Wave shuttle** is all you really need. One negative
about renting a car: parking is a bitch.

## THE WAVE
508-228-7025
www.nrtawave.com
The Wave is a **Shuttle Service** operated by the
Nantucket Regional Transit Authority (NRTA). It
takes people all over the island on various routes.

Some routes are served from 10 to 6 while on other routes service runs from 7 a.m. to 11:30 p.m. Tickets are cheap. If you're biking along and get tired, you can hop one of these and load your bike on the racks provided on the shuttle.

# Chapter 3
# WHERE TO STAY

**21 BROAD HOTEL**
21 Broad St, Nantucket, 508-228-4749
www.21broadhotel.com
This chic, Colonial-style hotel features 27 guest rooms with modern furnishings and luxury perks. Though the design nods to the typical Nantucket design elements you find everywhere on the island, this place is definitely much more modern. Lots of bright colors, giving the place a very uplifting atmosphere. You can hang out at their cold-pressed-juice bar during the day and then gather round the fire pit at night. It's right near the ferry landing and smack dab in the middle of the island's restaurant and bar scene. Amenities: Vitamin C shower, LED Smart TV, iPod docking station, complimentary Wi-Fi and breakfast. Hotel features: Back deck with fire pit and spa. Conveniently located 4 minutes from the Steamship Authority ferry terminal.

## THE BEACHSIDE AT NANTUCKET

30 North Beach St, Nantucket, 508-228-2241
www.thebeachside.com
This hotel offers 90 air-conditioned rooms and suites
including 6 pet-friendly rooms. Amenities include:
26" TVs, DVD player, cable TV, free wireless
Internet, free continental breakfast, and DVD library.
Facilities include outdoor heated swimming pool,
fitness center and free parking. All rooms are non-
smoking. Conveniently located close to Nantucket
Town and Jetties Beach.


## BRASS LANTERN NANTUCKET

11 North Water St, Nantucket, 800-377-6609
www.brasslanternnantucket.com
Located in the Old Historic District, this hotel offers
17 air-conditioned guestrooms and suites. Amenities

include: free Continental breakfast, pet friendly rooms and canopy beds. Conveniently located just a short walk from the ferry terminals, the **Whaling Museum,** local shopping and restaurants.

**LIFE HOUSE (formerly CENTURY HOUSE)**
10 Cliff Road, Nantucket, 866-466-7534
www.lifehousehotels.com/hotels/new-england/nantucket
Built in 1833, this luxury bed and breakfast offers beautiful renovated guestrooms. A verandah wraps around the place so there's always a nice place to sit and catch the ubiquitous breezes coming off the water. Amenities include: flat screen TVs, private baths, cable TV, DVD/CD player, book and DVD

library, free buffet breakfast, free fresh baked chocolate chip cookies, and free Wi-Fi. Century House offers a beautiful historic location with a wrap-around veranda, patio, and gardens. Conveniently located near local shopping, beaches, and restaurants.

**CLIFFSIDE BEACH CLUB**
46 Jefferson Ave, Nantucket, 508-228-0618
www.cliffsidebeach.com
This boutique hotel with its own private beach club offers guest 22 charming rooms and suites. Amenities include: free wireless Internet, flat screen TVs, and coffee makers. Rooms are all non-smoking. Facilities include: exercise and spa facility, private bar & café,

and pool. Located just one mile from the center of
Nantucket's town where guests can enjoy the local
shopping and restaurants.

## COTTAGES & LOFTS AT THE BOAT BASIN
24 Old South Wharf, Nantucket, 508-325-1378
www.thecottagesnantucket.com
These cottages and lofts offer a unique seaside
experience with 24 waterfront cottages and five new
deluxe lofts. Guests can enjoy waterfront views, full
kitchens and free bicycles. Amenities include: HD
Flat screen TVs, air conditioning, free Wi-Fi, free
Pre-Arrival concierge service robes and slippers. Pet
friendly lodging. Guests receive discounts at sister
hotel restaurants. In-room massages available. Non-
smoking property. Free Beach Bus.

## GREYDON HOUSE
17 Broad St, Nantucket, 508-228-2468
www.greydonhouse.com

Located in the downtown historic district in an 1850 Greek Revival building and just a 5-minute walk from the ferry, this new boutique hotel offers 18 luxurious guestrooms and suites. Unlike the typical Nantucket design elements, these people have added a lot of modern twists that are very refreshing. Neither the hotel nor the restaurant are priced as low as some of the more "thrifty' Nantucket regulars are used to, but so what? Splurge for once! Amenities: Complimentary mini bar, continental breakfast, toiletries, and flat-screen TV. On-site internationally inspired restaurant has local favorites with an Asian twist (like yuzu-roasted cod fish). Conveniently located just 18 minutes (walking) from the beach and near the Nantucket Whaling Museum, ferry docks and local shopping.

**THE JARED COFFIN HOUSE**
29 Broad St, Nantucket, 508-228-2400
www.jaredcoffinhouse.com

The Jared Coffin House, an historic in comprised of the Main House mansion and the Daniel Webster House, offers a variety of comfortable guest rooms with lots of dark woods, printed wallpapers, antiques in the public rooms. Built in 1845 by Jared Coffin, one of the most successful ship owners during the island's prime whaling days, this splendid three-story mansion was constructed in the center of town as his family's residence. It was the first such "mansion" ever built on the New England island.
(Has an excellent in-house restaurant, **Nantucket Prime**, primarily a steakhouse offering prime cuts of dry-aged and wet-aged beef, but it also has excellent fish dishes and a raw bar. There's also a 6-seat Chef's Table offering 2 seatings per night for the chef's 7-course meal.)  Amenities include: HD Flat screen TVs, free parking, free Wi-Fi, computer and printer access, free morning coffee and breakfast pastries, free afternoon coffee and cookies, free bottled water, book and magazine library, and Spa Access at the White Elephant.

**NANTUCKET HOTEL & RESORT**
77 Easton St, Nantucket, 508-228-4747
www.thenantuckethotel.com
Located 2 blocks from Children's Beach, this grand historic hotel offers a variety of guestrooms, suites, and private cottages. Very good for large parties—they have suites that sleep 11 or 15 persons. Amenities: Complimentary Wi-Fi, flat-screen TVs, private bathrooms, and coffeemakers. Hotel features: 2 seasonal heated pools, a hot tub, fitness center, and a casual restaurant with a year-round deck. Perks

include seasonal shuttle service to the ferry and local beaches. Walking distance to beaches, shopping, restaurants, and the harbor.

## SUMMER HOUSE COTTAGES

17 Ocean Ave, Nantucket, 508-257-4577
www.thesummerhouse.com
Overlooking the ocean, the Summer House is a boutique collection of inns and restaurants. The hotel features country-style rooms with marble bathrooms, wood floors and vintage furniture. Amenities: Complimentary Wi-Fi (no TVs) and breakfast. Hotel perks: a chic bistro right on the beach, a posh restaurant with patio dining and a piano bar. Freshwater outdoor pool. Complimentary jitney.

## THE SUMMER HOUSE INDIA STREET

31 India St, Nantucket, 508-257-4577
www.indiastreetinn.com **WEBSITE DOWN AT PRESSTIME**
The Summer House, located in the same collection as the Summer House Cottages, offers luxury accommodations. Guests enjoy staying in the restored whaling captain's mansion which includes a beautiful private garden and patio. Amenities: Complimentary Wi-Fi and breakfast. Private beach and pool access. Complimentary shuttle and jitney. Conveniently located near Maria Mitchell Aquarium and Jetties Beach.

## UNION STREET INN

7 Union St, Nantucket, 508-228-9222
www.unioninn.com
This intimate boutique inn offers 12 elegant
guestrooms. Amenities include: MALIN+GOETZ
bath amenities, flat screen TVs, and free Wi-Fi. Some
of the guest rooms feature wood-burning fireplaces.
This is the only Nantucket B&B serving a full
cooked-to-order breakfast. Afternoon treats include:
white chocolate chip cookies with macadamia nuts
and carrot cake.

## THE WAUWINET INN

120 Wauwinet Rd, Nantucket, 800-426-8718
www.wauwinet.com

Nestled between the Atlantic Ocean and Nantucket Bay, this boutique inn offers charming lodgings with 32 guest rooms and four cottages set across from the Main Inn. The Wauwinet is the only hotel on the island that's a member of Relais & Chateaux. This place has it all. Amenities include: Plush cotton robes, aroma therapy bath products, HD flat-screen TVs with premium channels, CD/DVD players, free Wi-Fi, free bottled water, free Continental breakfast, free coffee and fresh baked goods for early risers, free fruit anytime, daily newspaper, and DVD library. Non-smoking property.

## THE WHITE ELEPHANT
50 Easton St, Nantucket, 800-445-6574
www.whiteelephanthotel.com
An island landmark since the 1920s, this historic hotel offers 67 rooms including guest rooms, suites, garden cottages and in-town lofts. They started off with just a few harbor cottages and have grown over the years to offer a much wider variety of lodgings. At the popular **Brant Point Grill** located here, you can drink the White Elephant Ale named after this place made by the local **Cisco Brewery** over on Bartlett Park road. Amenities include: free high-speed Wi-Fi, Cable TV, DVD player, HD flat-screen TVs, radio/CD player, bottle water, beach towels, and beach chairs. Most rooms have outdoor patios and decks.

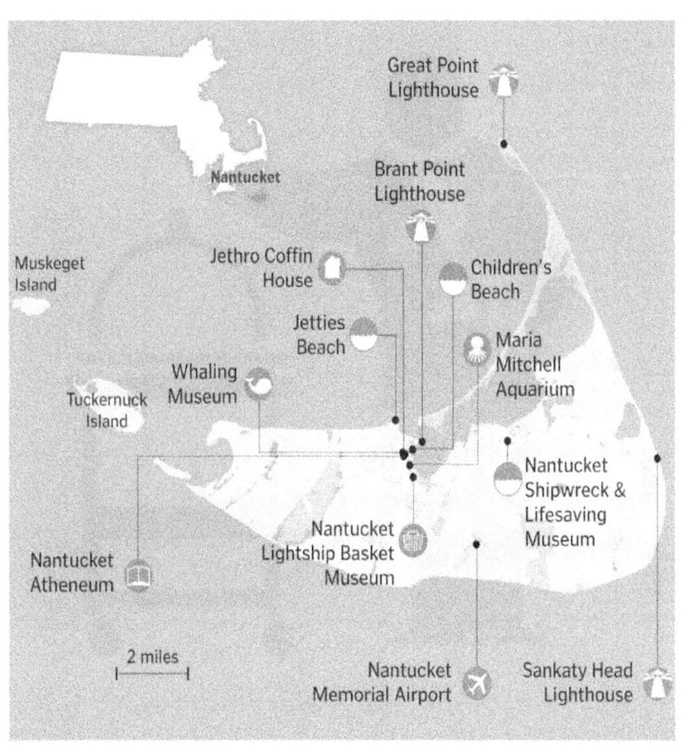

Nantucket
Muskeget
Island
Tuckernuck
Island
Great Point
Lighthouse
Brant Point
Lighthouse
Jethro Coffin
House
Children's
Beach
Jetties
Beach
Maria
Mitchell
Aquarium
Whaling
Museum
Nantucket
Shipwreck &
Lifesaving
Museum
Nantucket
Atheneum
Nantucket
Lightship Basket
Museum
2 miles
Nantucket
Memorial Airport
Sankaty Head
Lighthouse

# Chapter 4
## WHERE TO EAT

**AMERICAN SEASONS**
80 Center St, Nantucket, 508-228-7111
www.americanseasons.com
CUISINE: American (New)

DRINKS: Full Bar
SERVING: Dinner
PRICE RANGE: $$$
A little house located in a residential neighborhood, this eatery offers a great selection of American cuisine with a particular focus on regional foods. Favorites: Chicken liver mouse and Baked Salmon. Delicious desserts like Chocolate sorbet. Nice wine selection.

**B-ACK Yard BBQ**
20 Straight Wharf, Nantucket, 508-228-0227
https://ackbackyard.com/
CUISINE: Barbecue/American
DRINKS: Full Bar
SERVING: Lunch & Dinner

PRICE RANGE: $$
Bare-bones, no frills sports bar serving the tastiest authentic barbecue with a Nantucket twist. Favorites: Dry Rub Wings and Pulled Pork. Impressive selection of Kentucky bourbons, Tennessee whiskeys, and craft beer. Cocktails are the stars here with names like Stevie Ray, and Georgia on My Mind.

**B-ACK YARD BBQ (above)**

**BARTLETT'S FARM**
33 Bartlett Farm Rd, Nantucket, 508-228-9403
www.bartlettsfarm.com
CUISINE: Grocery/Sandwiches/Breakfast

DRINKS: No Booze
SERVING: 8 a.m. – 7 p.m.
PRICE RANGE: $$
Grocery that also offers a great selection of sandwiches and prepared entrees and sides. Foods offered include: Bacon Lentil Salad, Pasta Primavera Salad, Tomato Salad, Grilled Organic Chicken Breasts, Rigatoni Marinara, Raw Slaw, and Cous Cous (just to name a few). The homemade chicken salad is excellent. Try their White Chocolate & Raspberry Bread Pudding – so good. Hot lunch specials are offered daily from September through May. Breads are made by a quality supplier here on the island, **Something Natural**, which is also a good place to stop for sandwiches, by the way.
http://somethingnatural.com/

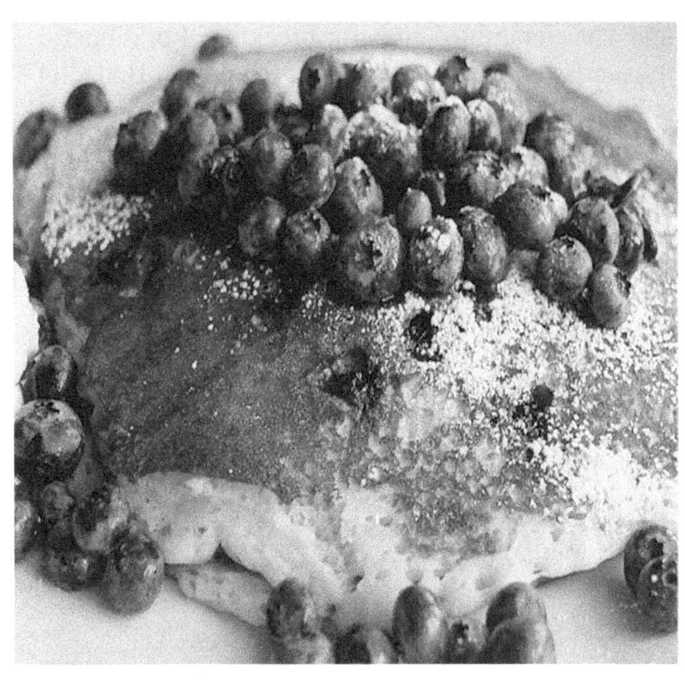

## BLACK-EYED SUSANS

10 India Street, 508-325-0308
www.black-eyedsusans.com
CUISINE: American
DRINKS: No Booze; BYOB; modest corkage fee.
SERVING: Breakfast, Lunch, Dinner
PRICE RANGE: $$ / **cash only**
This little breakfast spot is a favorite of locals and
tourists. Great place for brunch but if you want a
mimosa or bloody Mary make sure to bring your own
booze. For dinner, they have 3 seatings, 6; 7:30 and
10. Indoors or outdoors. Choose one and make a
reservation. (Before, they'd only take reservations for
6, so be sure this doesn't change after we go to press.)
Menu favorites include: Curried eggs with broccoli

and Thai scrambled eggs for breakfast. For dinner, mustard-soy marinated salmon; local cod "Benedict style," with an egg poached in wine, Niman ranch ham and potatoes; pork scaloppini Marsala. It's really good here. Always busy.

**BOARDING HOUSE**
12 Federal St, Nantucket, 508-228-9622
www.boardinghousenantucket.com/
CUISINE: American (New)
DRINKS: Full Bar
SERVING: Dinner nightly, Lunch on Sat
PRICE RANGE: $$
Offering a distinctive menu of Mediterranean inspired New American dishes. This eatery, nicknamed BoHo, has earned many accolades, including Best Brunch. Sit out on the patio for the best views. Favorites:

Yellow Fin Tuna and Krack Crab stuffed avocado.
Popular spot for weekend brunch.


**BRANT POINT GRILL**
**WHITE ELEPHANT HOTEL**
50 Easton St, Nantucket, 508-325-1320
www.whiteelephanthotel.com
CUISINE: American
DRINKS: Full Bar
SERVING: Brunch, Lunch, Dinner
PRICE RANGE: $$$$
Located in the White Elephant Hotel, this grill is
known to locals as **BPG**. The American menu offers a
variety of fresh seafood, steaks and specialties like
the savory lobster dinner. Menu favorites include the
Grilled Salmon Salad. Their Sunday Brunch is
considered one of the best on the Island. Nice wine
selection. (They have a coveted Wine Spectator
Award for the excellence of their list.)

## BREEZE
### Nantucket Hotel & Resort

77 Easton St, Nantucket, 508-228-4730
https://www.thenantuckethotel.com/dining/breeze/
CUISINE: Seafood/American (New) / Int'l
DRINKS: Full Bar
SERVING: Breakfast, Lunch & Dinner
PRICE RANGE: $$$

Located in the award-winning Nantucket Hotel, this slightly upmarket fashionable eatery offers up a menu of contemporary international cuisine (but it's mostly typical Nantucket fare). Favorites: Lobster roll with truffle fries and Salmon Cesare salad. Try their infamous Flourless Chocolate cake. Dine indoors or out on the terrace by the glowing fire. Live entertainment during season.

## THE CHANTICLEER

9 New St, Siasconset, 508-257-4499
www.chanticleernantucket.com
CUISINE: American (New)
DRINKS: Full Bar
SERVING: Lunch & Dinner
PRICE RANGE: $$$
Upscale dining at its finest in elegant or casual dining rooms. The most charming is the area in the rose garden where you can dine. Menu consists mainly of fish and salads with special dishes like tuna tartar, swordfish and the Maine lobster. Also they have a burger made with a mixture of brisket, short ribs and

sirloin. Fair selection of wine. Book ahead at peak
season.

## COMPANY OF THE CAULDRON
5 India St, Nantucket, 508-228-4016
www.companyofthecauldron.com
CUISINE: American
DRINKS: Beer & Wine
SERVING: Lunch, early dinner
PRICE RANGE: $$$$
Located in the heart of the Historic District, this small
and romantic eatery offers a special fine dining
experience with an ever-changing prix fixe menu.
Menu favorites include: Herb & Ginger Crusted Rack

of Lamb and Grilled Sliced Flat Iron Steak. Extensive
wine list. Reservations needed.

**CRU**
1 Straight Wharf, Nantucket, 508-228-9278
www.crunantucket.com
CUISINE: Seafood/American (New)
DRINKS: Full Bar
SERVING: Lunch & Dinner
PRICE RANGE: $$
Stylish eatery located right on the water with a great
seafood selection. This is no beach bum waterfront
hangout. No, it's sophisticated, upscale and charming.
Raw bar. Favorites: Grilled Wester-Ross Salmon and
Haddock Schnitzel. Best lobster roll on the island.
(Well, hmm – OK, *one* of the best.) Crafted cocktails.

**DOWNYFLAKE**
18 Sparks Ave, Nantucket, 508-228-4533
www.thedownyflake.com

CUISINE: Sandwiches/American
DRINKS: No Booze
SERVING: Breakfast & Lunch
PRICE RANGE: $
Country café (all right, it's a great little dumpy diner)
known for their delicious housemade donuts. Great
breakfast spot – Smoked salmon and other breakfast
treats but don't think of leaving without getting one
of their donuts.

**DUNE**
20 Broad St, Nantucket, 508-228-5550
www.dunenantucket.com
CUISINE: American
DRINKS: Full Bar
SERVING: Dinner
PRICE RANGE: $$$
Created by Michael Getter (a longtime island chef),
this restaurant offers an ever-changing creative menu

of traditional American classics. Even though they have 3 rooms for dining, as well as an outdoor patio, plan on booking ahead. It's that good. (And that busy.) Menu favorites include: Sauteed Scottish Salmon and Lemon & Oregano Grilled Chicken. Nice dessert selection but chocolate lovers should try the Chocolate Sampler including: orange chocolate pot de creme, Mexican chocolate torte, coco mousse, and chocolate tiles. Nice wine list.

**EASY STREET CANTINA**
2 Broad St, Nantucket, 508-228-5418
www.easystreetcantina.com
CUISINE: Mexican-American
DRINKS: No Booze
SERVING: Breakfast & Lunch
PRICE RANGE: $
Right near the ferry, so if you're just arriving, fill up on some inexpensive food before you start touring the island. Has typical breakfast fare (which they serve all day) with some Mexican twists. Lots of New England standard fare like fried shrimp, fried clams, fish & chips, fried scallops—all of it quite good for a super price. Veggie burritos; fish and meat tacos; guacamole; taco salad. Indoor/outdoor seating. You order at the counter.

**GALLEY BEACH**
54 Jefferson Ave, Nantucket, 508-228-9641
www.galleybeach.net
CUISINE: Seafood
DRINKS: Full Bar

SERVING: Lunch, Dinner; weekend Brunch starts at 10 a.m.
PRICE RANGE: $$$$

Run by the same family since 1958, this restaurant is one of the island's premier restaurants and a favorite marriage location. It's exactly a mile out of town, right on the beach overlooking Nantucket Sound. (Ask anyone. They will point you in the right direction.) One of the more romantic setting on the whole island. In season, they have chairs and table right on the beach. This eatery is elegant yet casual and Chef Neil Ferguson offers a creative seafood menu. Menu favorites include: Lamb Chop with Braised Lamb Neck and Sea Scallops & Lobster; crispy sweetbreads; Atlantic halibut; fluke with braised fennel; roasted guinea fowl. Great sunset views through the wall of windows or at the bar on the beach.

## ISLAND KITCHEN

1 Chin's Way, Nantucket, 508-228-2639
https://www.nantucketislandkitchen.com/
CUISINE: American (New)/Seafood
DRINKS: Full Bar
SERVING: Breakfast (in season), Lunch & Dinner
PRICE RANGE: $$

Located in a shingled house, this small no-frills eatery with very basic blond wooden tables & matching wooden chairs serves the best breakfast on Nantucket (while the Breakfast BLT is really excellent, I generally get the hangar steak & eggs). Creative menu picks include Roasted Beet & Whipped Goat Cheese and the Spicy Tuna Bowl. For dessert they serve some of the best ice cream on the island.

## KEEPERS

5 Amelia Dr, Nantucket, 508-228-0009
https://www.keepersnantucket.com/
CUISINE: American (New)/Vegetarian friendly
DRINKS: Full Bar
SERVING: Dinner; Closed Wednesdays
PRICE RANGE: $$

Neighborhood restaurant where the locals eat all year.
Limited menu. Favorites include BLT salad with
chicken and Old Bay Butter Broiled Shrimp. Nice
selection of seafood.

## MILLIE'S

326 Madaket Rd, Nantucket, 508-228-8435
www.milliesnantucket.com
CUISINE: Tex-Mex
DRINKS: Full Bar
SERVING: Dinner
PRICE RANGE: $$

On the west end of the island is this place that is the perfect location for a sunset drink. (They have a second floor glassed-in area that gives you a great view.) Chef David Scribner offers a California Baja style menu featuring fresh local seafood, handmade salsa and guacamole, Po Boys and tacos. Menu favorites include: Steak Taco and Scallop Quesadilla. Children's Menu. Bar offers a nice menu of specialty cocktails, champagnes, and wines including some Nantucket labels from places like the **Cisco Brewery**.

# THE NAUTILUS
12 Cambridge St, Nantucket, 508-228-0301
www.nautilusnantucket.com
CUISINE: Tapas Bars/American (New) / Asian fusion
DRINKS: Full Bar
SERVING: Dinner
PRICE RANGE: $$$
Rustic-modern small plates restaurant with a menu focused on seafood. Favorites: Scallion pancakes, Oyster tacos and Green curry lobster. Great inventive craft cocktails like the tasty Barr Hill Gin Marini – their crown jewel.

## ORAN MOR

2 S Beach St, Nantucket, 508-228-8655
www.oranmorbistro.com
CUISINE: American (New)
DRINKS: Full Bar
SERVING: Dinner
PRICE RANGE: $$$
Located in a historic home, this is one of Nantucket's best, offering a creative menu of seasonal dishes, handcrafted cocktails and wines. Menu picks: Duck and Black truffle bucatini. Elegant dining experience.

## THE PEARL

12 Federal St, Nantucket, 508-228-9701
www.thepearlnantucket.com
CUISINE: Seafood
DRINKS: Full Bar
SERVING: Dinner

PRICE RANGE: $$$$
Upscale eatery offering a creative Asian Fusion menu. Menu picks: Fried Lobster and Sweet & Sour Halibut. Delicious desserts. Reservations necessary.

## THE PROPRIETORS BAR & TABLE
9 India St, Nantucket, 508-228-7477
www.proprietorsnantucket.com
CUISINE: American
DRINKS: Full Bar
SERVING: Dinner
PRICE RANGE: $$$
Chef Tom Berry offers an interesting menu of small and large plate dishes. Menu favorites include: Grass Fed Bavette Steak and Carolina Spatchcock. The wine list offers a curated selection of international bottles from the Old and New World. Interesting desserts for sweet lovers like the Strawberry Mess, a strawberry and cream concoction.

## PROVISIONS

3 Harbor Square, Straight Wharf, Nantucket, 508-228-3258

https://provisions-nantucket.com/

CUISINE: American

DRINKS: No Booze

SERVING: Lunch, early dinner

PRICE RANGE: $$ / Cash Only

Excellent, reasonably priced sandwich shop on an island known for how expensive everything is. Provisions is famous for its Turkey Terrific Sandwich. I'll tell you why it's so terrific. They cut the turkey real thick and they have a special cranberry sauce that's to die for. But their Caprese Sandwich has to come in second. (Mouthwatering mozzarella and tomatoes.) You order at the counter and they bring your sandwiches to your table. Obviously, they do a lot of take-out here for people just getting off the

ferry or just getting on. Great place to pick up a snack
for the ferry ride back to the mainland.

## QUEEQUEG'S
6 Oak St, Nantucket, 508-325-0992
http://queequegsnantucket.com/
CUISINE: American (New)/Seafood
DRINKS: Full Bar
SERVING: Lunch & Dinner
PRICE RANGE: $$$
Comfortable eatery with indoor (cozy with dark wood
everywhere) and outdoor dining under umbrellas with
twinkle lights. Favorites include Caprese salad,
Shrimp Scampi, and Short Ribs. Reservations
recommended.

Inside The Sea Grille, darker and cozier (Above)

**SEA GRILLE**
45 Sparks Ave, Nantucket Ma, 508-325-5700
http://www.theseagrille.com/
CUISINE: American/Seafood/Vegetarian Friendly
DRINKS: Full Bar
SERVING: Lunch & Dinner
PRICE RANGE: $$$$
A locals' favorite with a creative menu of seafood
and meat dishes. Homemade lobster tortellini; Bacon
Wrapped Scallops, and Clam Fritters are all my
absolute favorites. Reservations recommended.

Sea Grille out on the porch. (Above)

**SHIP'S INN**
13 Fair St, Nantucket, 508-228-0040
www.shipsinnnantucket.com
CUISINE: Bed & Breakfast
DRINKS: Beer & Wine
SERVING: Lunch & Dinner
PRICE RANGE: $$
Bed & Breakfast serving lunch and dinner. Favorites: Halibut in morel sauce and Swordfish. Vegetarian options available. Another thing that'll impress you is the wonderful selection of breads served at beginning of the meal.

**SLIP 14**
14 Old S Wharf, Nantucket, 508-228-2033
www.slip14.com
CUISINE: American (New)
DRINKS: Full Bar
SERVING: Lunch & Dinner
PRICE RANGE: $$
Comfortable eatery offering a fish-focused menu.
Favorites: Lobster mac n cheese and Cornmeal
Crusted Calamari. Creative cocktails. Great wine
selection. Water views.

## SUMMER HOUSE RESTAURANT

17 Ocean Ave, Siasconset, 508-257-9976
www.thesummerhouse.com
CUISINE: American
DRINKS: Full Bar
SERVING: Breakfast, Lunch, Dinner
PRICE RANGE: $$$

With a beautiful Siasconset location, this eatery from
Chef Todd English offers a nice contemporary
American menu and impressive wine list. Menu
favorites include: char-grilled swordfish; poached
lobster salad with green beans; lobster fra diavola.
Live piano with sing-alongs. A good alternative to the
dining room is their **Beachside Bistro** where you can
have lunch under an umbrella and take in the breeze.

## TOPPER'S TIDBITS
## THE WAUWINET
120 Wauwinet Rd, Nantucket, 508-228-8768
www.wauwinet.com
CUISINE: American
DRINKS: Full bar
SERVING: Breakfast, Lunch, Dinner
PRICE RANGE: $$$

One of the best restaurants on the island, Topper's serves Retsyo Oysters, which are harvested just 300 yards from the Wauwinet. Seasonally inspired menu featuring excellent seafood specialties. (There's a deck where you can get a more casual menu, and the bar always makes a good place to stop by.) Wine Spectator Grand Award for its wine list carrying over 1,500 labels.

## VENTUNO

21 Federal St, Nantucket, 508-228-4242
www.ventunorestaurant.com
CUISINE: Italian
DRINKS: Full Bar
SERVING: Dinner
PRICE RANGE: $$$

Located in a Greek revival building, this elegant eatery offers Italian classics with a twist. Try to get a table on the patio outside because they have one of the most appealing on the whole island. Fresh homemade pastas make you think you're in Italy.

# Chapter 5
# NIGHTLIFE

## CHICKEN BOX
16 Dave St (just off Lower Orange St), Nantucket,
508-228-9717
www.thechickenbox.com
This popular bar is a longtime favorite of locals and
tourists. Here you'll find a revolving schedule of live
music, pool tables, foosball, darts, and cheap drinks.
Outdoor area for smoking and lounging. Cover after 9

p.m. Very busy on weekends and there's usually a line at the door.

## CLUB CAR

1 Main St, Nantucket, 508-228-1101
www.theclubcar.com
The Club Car is a railway car transformed into a restaurant and lounge. This place always attracts a crowd with its live music and popular bar scene. Serves lunch and dinner, too.

## GALLEY BEACH

54 Jefferson Ave, Nantucket, 508-228-9641
www.galleybeach.net
Though it's primarily a restaurant, a cool crowd of hipsters come together here in the back room in the evenings, making this a great place to go out. Stay inside or hang out on the sand where they put our comfortable couches and flaming torches provide light. Excellent craft cocktails.

**KITTY MURTAUGH'S**
4 West Creek Rd, Nantucket, 508-228-0781
www.kittymurtaghs.com
This place offers two levels, and Irish pub upstairs
and an intimate dining room downstairs. Decorated
with Irish signs and antiques, this place feels like an
authentic Irish pub. Upstairs enjoy a mug of Guinness
and downstairs enjoy authentic Irish fare.

# Chapter 6
# WHAT TO SEE & DO

**HY-LINE CRUISES**
34 Straight Wharf, Nantucket, 508-228-3949
www.hylinecruises.com
This is a passenger-only cruise line traveling between
Nantucket and Hyannis. Moderate rate. Cruises

leaving several times daily. Deep-sea fishing cruises are also available.

## MARIA MITCHELL ASSOCIATION
4 Vestal St, Nantucket, 508-228-9198
www.mariamitchell.org
This is a private non-profit organization founded in 1902 to preserve the legacy of Maria Mitchell, an astronomer, naturalist, librarian and educator. The association operates two observatories, a natural science museum, an aquarium, and the historic birthplace of Maria Mitchell. **BIRD TOURS**: They also offer tours highlighting the island's rich bird population. You get to visit places that are not crowded like **Eel Point**, which you get to either on foot or in a 4-wheel drive vehicle. See if you can spot a sharp-tailed sparrow in the salt marshes. The association offers science and history-related programing. Admission fees at various venues.

## NANTUCKET FARMERS & ARTISANS MARKET

Cambridge and North Union Streets, 508-228-3399
www.sustainablenantucket.org
This sustainable Farmers and Artisans Market is at
several locations: Downtown on Saturdays and the
Muse Parking lot (44 Surfside Road) on Tuesdays
from July through August. The 60-odd vendors
include growers, artisans, and prepared food
purveyors. Get a Flip Flop Quilt from or quilted
backpacks from **Island Quilts**. Or a handwoven
Alpaca Houndstooth Throw from **Island Weaves**. Or
pendants, necklaces, rings and other jewelry from
**Keely Smith Designs**. Most of the vendors have
stores elsewhere on Nantucket, so if you're not here
during the market, you can visit the individual stores.
The market also includes live music performances,
kids' activities, and demonstrations.

## NANTUCKET ISLAND TOURS

Various locations, Nantucket, 508-228-0334
https://www.nantucketbustours.com/
This company offers fully narrated tours of Nantucket
Island. The tour, which takes just over an hour,
introduces you to the "Little Grey Lady," as
Nantucket is known, which was the world's foremost
whaling port in the 18$^{th}$ century. The tour includes:
The Old Mill, "Sconset" Village, Low Beach,
Sankaty Head Lighthouse, Cranberry bogs and
Nantucket moors. The tours operate from May
through October. Reservations needed.

## THE NANTUCKET REGIONAL TRANSIT AUTHORITY

20-R S. Water St, Nantucket, 508-228-7025
www.nrtawave.com

NRTA offers island wide shuttle and van service. Island wide service includes nine routes with 13 buses.

## NANTUCKET SHIPWRECK & LIFESAVING MUSEUM
158 Polpis Rd, Nantucket, 508-228-2505
www.nantucketshipwreck.org
This museum celebrates the memory of the islanders who risked their lives to save shipwrecked mariners like the Massachusetts Humane Society, United States Life-Saving Service and the United States Coast Guard. There are over 700 documented wrecks

in the difficult waters surrounding Nantucket, and this is the place to relive some of that history. A special treat here is some eerie film footage of the Italian liner "Andrea Doria" as she lists to her side after being struck broadside in a fogbank off Nantucket by the Swedish liner "Stockholm."   The museum features revolving exhibitions, films, family-friendly programs and special events. Nominal fee.

## THE OLD MILL
50 Prospect Street, Nantucket, 508-228-1894
www.nha.org/sites/oldmill.html#_=_
Built in 1746 by Nathan Wilbur,
This "Old Mill" is the oldest functioning mill in the U.S. At one time there were four "smock mills" that overlooked Nantucket town however this is the only remaining mill. Nominal fee. Tour available.

## PETER FOULGER MUSEUM
15 Broad St, Nantucket, 508-228-1894
www.nha.org
This museum exhibits paintings, furniture, and other items illustrating the island's rich history. Nominal fee.

## THE QUAKER MEETINGHOUSE
7 Fair St, Nantucket, 508-228-1894
www.nha.org/sites/quakermeetinghouse.html
This site celebrates the early days of the Quakers in
the years after 1708. This meetinghouse was erected
in 1832 and originally served as a school for the
Wilburite Sect. In the 1940s the Quakers began
meeting here again. This was the first museum of the
Nantucket Historical Association. Nominal fee. Tours
available.

## SHEARWATER EXCURSIONS
Straight Wharf, Nantucket, 508-228-7037
www.explorenantucket.com
This is a family-run, year-round eco-tour company
that offers tours of the many ecosystems in the

Nantucket area and also the underdeveloped outer islands of Tuckernuck and Muskeget. These excursions provide a great educational adventure with narration. Two ferry lines run between Hyannis and Nantucket several times daily during the summer. Moderate fee for six-hour excursion.

## THE STEAMSHIP AUTHORITY
508- 477-8600
www.steamshipauthority.com
This is the largest ferry service that travels to the Islands of Martha's Vineyard and Nantucket from Cape Cod. Frequent daily departures are offered for passengers, groups, autos, and trucks. Travel dock to dock in just an hour. Spacious seating on board with snack bars, free Wi-Fi and TV.

## TIDAL CREEKS SHIP STORE
32 Washington St, Nantucket, 508-228-6244
https://tidalcreeksshipstore.com/
This is the island's one-stop-shopping for boat sales, new and used, as well as trailers, hardware, batteries, repair supplies, electronics equipment, paints, varnishes, safety equipment, foul weather gear, and all types of boating wear. Exclusive Island dealer for Casco Bay Skiffs, Sea Pro, Bristol Skiffs, and Zodiac. **Shellfish Permits** are available at the harbormaster's office next door. You can harvest soft-shell clams on the mud flats until the middle of June, but quahogs are good year-round. Get the waders, racks, gloves and a basket here at Tidal Creeks Marine.

## TRIPLE EIGHT DISTILLERY
## CISCO BREWERS
## NANTUCKET VINEYARD

5 Bartlett Farm Road, Nantucket, 508-325-5929
www.ciscobrewers.com
This operation has evolved from a winery initially to
include a brewery as well as a distillery where they
make spirits. The tours are especially interesting.

## WHALING MUSEUM
13 Broad St, Nantucket, 508-228-1894
www.nha.org
This museum primarily exhibits its large collection of whaling artifacts and memorabilia. The centerpiece of the museum's collection is a complete skeleton of a 45-foot bull whale that is suspended from the ceiling. Other highlights include an 1849 Fresnel lens used in the **Sankaty Head Lighthouse** and workings of the 1881 town clock. There's a big collection of artifacts from the doomed ship "Essex," which was struck (and sunk) by a sperm whale it was chasing. (Sounds like the plot of "Moby Dick," doesn't it? It ought to. That real-life story inspired Herman Melville to write the book, which I find impossible to read.) The building housing the museum was a candle factory a century ago. Nominal admission fee. Nantucket Historical Association located on the second level.

# Chapter 7
## SHOPPING & SERVICES

**CHRISTOPHER WHEAT**
585-329-8997
www.christopherwheat.com
Wheat paints all sorts of island scenes and is highly
regarded in these parts for his work.

## ERICA WILSON

25 Main St, Nantucket, 508-228-9881
www.ericawilson.com
Hip boutique offering women's and children's fashions. Also available are bracelets, accent jewelry, needlework canvases and supplies.

## HENLEY & SLOANE

18A Federal St, Nantucket, 508-228-6209
www.henleyandsloane.com
Men's clothing featuring the finest traditional English shirt makers and clothiers. Flawless designs and tailoring. They are justly famous for their striped socks. Make sure you get a couple of pairs.

## MILLY & GRACE

2 Washington St, Nantucket, 508-901-5051
www.millyandgrace.com
Set in a little ivy covered building, this shop offers feminine and vintage inspired fashions and home décor. Here you'll find everything from flirty dresses to cashmere, jewelry and beautiful home décor. The shop was named after the owners' grandmothers.

## MITCHELL'S BOOK CORNER

54 Main St, Nantucket, 508-228-1080
www.mitchellsbookcorner.com
This is a full service, independent bookstore that's
been here for over 40 years boasting an extensive
selection of books numbering in the thousands about
Nantucket, whaling, history of the island, and a stock
of titles in all genres. Has lots of readings by visiting
authors, other activities.

## MURRAY'S TOGGERY SHOP

62 Main St, Nantucket, 508-228-0437
www.nantucketreds.com
This store stocks a variety of clothing and gifts from
around the world including: Nantucket Red's Pants,
shorts, shirts, and jewelry. Brands carried include:
Bill's Khakis, Castaway Clothing, Diane Reilly
Jewelry, Eliza B, Hatley, La Soula, Lacoste,
Leatherman, New England Nauticals, Peter Millar,
Smathers & Branson, and Southern Tide.

**NANTUCKET BOOKWORKS**

25 Broad Street, Nantucket, 508-228-4000
www.nantucketbookpartners.com
This funky little bookshop is stocked with great
books, toys, gifts, cards and local music. An excellent
place to stop in to browse the hundreds of books
about Nantucket. Nice lavish coffeetable books, too.
The owner says her bestseller is Nathaniel Philbrick's
book from 2000, "In the Heart of the Sea," which
recounts the tragedy of the "Essex," a whaling ship
struck and sunk by a sperm whale in 1820 in the
South Pacific. you can see some artifacts in the
**Whaling Museum**.

**NANTUCKET LOOMS**

51 Main St, Nantucket, 508-228-1908
www.nantucketlooms.com
Known the world over since they opened in 1968 for
their textiles, hand-woven throws and beautiful one-
of-a-kind mohair and cashmere creations. Women
love this place. Home furnishings and accessories.
Interior design services available.

## SUNKEN SHIP

12 Broad St, Nantucket, 508-228-9226
www.sunkenship.com
Retail shop offering huge selection of t-shirts, hats,
sweatshirts, souvenirs, and almost anything you're
looking for. Also available: scuba lessons, tank fills,
diving equipment, and dive charters. It's been here
since 1975 and the island wouldn't be the same
without it.

## SUSTAINABLE NANTUCKET'S FARMERS & ARTISANS MARKET

Various locations
www.sustainablenantucket.org
Farmers & Artisans market features a vast selection
from local growers, food producers, and artisans.
Great place to begin the day with breakfast before
lunging into the wide variety of offerings here. Go to
Wicked Island Bakery for coffee and one of their
mouthwatering breakfast buns:
http://wickedislandbakery.com/
You'll find everything including: organically grown
seasonal produce, honey, handmade Italian cheeses,
jewelry, photography, glass art, t-shirts, soap, and
flowers. Live music, kids' activity tables and
demonstrations. Check website for location.

## YOUNG'S BICYCLE SHOP

6 Broad St, Nantucket, 508-228-1151
www.youngsbicycleshop.com
This is your one-stop-shopping destination for bikes and bike gear. They sell, rent, and service bikes. They also offer car and jeep rentals.

# INDEX